THE POETRY BOOK ABOUT M.E.: MELANIN EXPERIENCE

BY: CHANEKKA PULLENS

Contact Information:

Email: Mindelevationforall@gmail.com

The Poetry Book About M.E.: Melanin Experience

© 2016 Chanekka Pullens. All Rights Reserved.

Cover art created by Yahonatan Yisra'el

No part of this book may be reproduced or transmitted in any form or by any means, written, electronic, recording, photocopying, or otherwise, without prior written permission of the author, Chanekka LuQuawn Pullens.

Books may be purchased in quantity and/or special sales by contacting the author by email at: Mindelevationforall@gmail.com , with "Book Purchase" in the subject line.

ISBN: 978-0-692-77716-9

1. Motivation 2. Inspiration 3. Poetry

First Edition

Printed in the USA

Dedicated to every black soul that was taken without cause.

"Strength takes control, the ability, and the consistency to outweigh the obstacle at hand. No storm lasts forever."

– Chanekka Pullens

INTRODUCTION

When you're young you have all of these ideas about how you want your life to be. You have dreams and goals, but you never really know how life is going to play out for you. You never really know what GOD has planned for you or what's marked for your days ahead. When we were growing up we didn't have much but we had each other. Regardless of our environment and surroundings, we made the best of it. We had good times and bad times, but overall we learned to survive. We know what it's like to struggle that why we're so appreciative and humbled of our successes.

Growing up the way I grew up was hard. I was in foster care from 2 1/2 months old until I was 17 years old. Being without my parents was extremely hard; but my grandmother always told me," Things that happen in your life are either blessings or lessons". So I took their absence as a lesson on what not to do. I'm just blessed that I had my sisters and my brother to lean on. I don't know what I would've done without them. I know I can always count on them for support.

My melanin experience hasn't been an easy one but I'm blessed in spite of the downfalls. I'm so happy to contribute my words and passion in this book. I am so proud of you Chaé! I'm proud of the woman you've become. I'm proud of your growth both spiritually and mentally. I'm proud of you for being as strong as you are and most of all I'm proud to call you my sister. You are truly an inspiration to not only me but everyone you come in contact with. Never let anybody dim your light and remember pressure makes diamonds. You wear your crown well Queen!

Love your sister,

    Tiesha McKenzie

BELIEVE

See I was born in the land of poplar trees.

Home of the slaves.

Place of the 'we don't give a fuck' generation

so we misbehave.

Oppression in my bones,

jail cell bound.

Project buildings built on Indian burial grounds.

I'm the offspring of the struggle.

Manufactured by the streets.

I'm the pretty brown rose that grew from the concrete.

Melanin covered, skin rich like Shea butter.

And you tell me that Black dope fiends

aren't queens? Thugs aren't kings?

But what do you have to hold on to

when the pipe takes your dream?

And the atmosphere around you is choking your self-esteem?

BELIEVE that you can ELEVATE above anything.

BELIEVE that even when you're sleep walking you can dream.

    -Tiesha McKenzie

BORN

Born in 1990 into sin.

Born into a race with no wins.

Born, into a place, where he would never be noticed.

Evil planted, and grew, and stirred into a potion.

Witchcraft, curses blowing in the wind.

His first breath deemed him doomed, he was sent.

Straight to the bottom, expected to lose every challenge.

But he was strong in his mind, even color blind.

He saw not, black or white, only grey.

Didn't love one more than the other, his heart did not segregate.

Yet, twenty-three years and a month, on the eighth day.

He was, faced, yet with another challenge.

Begged the white man not to shoot, that he had a family.

But, only seeing someone with a black face,

pulled the trigger and said, "Nigger". Heart full of implanted hate.

And to this day, I forgive those who took part,

in ending my brother, a life they didn't start.

Don't understand how a man, can have so much power.

Power could have been mine, instead I stood by my bible.

Won't let this world, contaminate my body or my mind.

Raising his two kids on the principle, think about the reciprocal.

If you were in his shoes, would you want it did to you?

No? Well, don't do it to him.

Don't only see black and white, no 20's film.

Feed the truth and beauty, a righteous meal.

Rest in peace, Kenny, your lives here will

prosper!

I pray they don't be killed because of their color.

Amen!

CHALLENGES OF THE BODY

Burning rage.

Flames, temperature rising in my blood and veins.

White blood cells turning to stone, heart gets separated,

Because it's frozen as if Ulsa, pointed her fingers in its direction.

It's stuck in a perception, that it's hidden behind the outer reputation.

Steady waiting to matter.

Ears, become deaf to the chatter,

to the deceit, to the lies.

Eyes, afraid to see tomorrow, but curious...

So they're wide open but blind.

Nose, only smells the scent of coffins and cells,

of trees with no leaves, flat irons on weave.

Hands, can only feel, for hope that's far away.

Hands touched my brother lifeless three years ago, still feel him today.

Soul remains hopeful, dedicated to a self-promise.

For a world of equality, acceptance, and understanding.

Of that that makes one different,

Unique, Special.

So, soon the flames in my blood and veins will subside,

white cells will come to life, and heart reattached.

It will beat again, because it will be seen beyond the color of my skin.

Ears will listen to the truth,

Eyes will look forward to tomorrow,

Nose will smell victory.

Hands will make a difference and feel hope and prosperity.

Soul will be proud that it never swayed during,

The challenges of the body.

NO MORE

Imagine,

Pressure from the streaming waters pressing against, contained glass.

Pressure from the wind blowing aggressively against, contained glass.

Lightening from the sky striking millions of times against, contained glass.

Now imagine,

A vessel,

which contains the pressure from the streaming waters, blowing winds and lightening

holding firm for years.

The surface on which the vessel stands, is swayed by these forces,

Yet, the vessel stands.

Picture,

as these pressures continue with the surface rocking

for years, continue, with none of these stopping.

Can you imagine?

Will it be okay if the top began to loosen and reality was confusing;

And life was in question, when nothing was protected; And

faith wasn't enough, and the pressure in my gut said.

It was okay to scream.

Would it be?

Maybe if I did so just once,

followed the pressure in my gut.

Let out this scream!

The pressure will be no more.

REVEALS

She reveals her vessel to every eye that's laid upon her.

Her birthmarks are no secret, no part of her is a mystery.

There is no need for imagination, when they see this girl.

I would say lady, but a lady keeps her secrets from the world.

This girl, has no purity inside of her intimately,

She's open for business, for any witness

who wishes.

Well says, they want to get to know her.

On the stage, she twerks, on the inside she hurts.

To hide the fact that she was broken, at every turn.

Around this monopoly board she's the dog piece that chases the money bag.

Meaning, if he goes to jail or files for bankruptcy, she's right behind.

She invested in her body, but when illness falls, and no shot or surgery can

lift up or bump out,

What will be left?

When the heels break, and the poles rust,

 What will be left?

If there was only one man on earth, who finds a queen with secrets

Will you be able to survive?

Opposites don't always attract.

If the dog chases the money bag, who do you think will be chasing her back?

The dog.

Because a dog smells ass a dog's ass, and that's how they show their amusement.

You'll both be waiting on the postman together, wondering where the news went.

Mayday!! Mayday!! Not sure where respect is.

Think of the title of the story, and if you consider this boring,

Just think of your secrets and how many knows.

If nine out of ten does,

Well, there you go!

WHAT MATTERS

(Takes a deep breath)

STOP!

I close my eyes, try to stop the ground from shaking.

Trying not to fall between the cracks, into the endless abyss.

Of nothing. Of emptiness.

Of a place where it was meant for me to be.

I stand firm and confident of the idea of better days.

The idea that the ground will stop shaking and the cracks become united.

This current state, can't wait another day. Especially two.

But what it can do, is move toward the better days, and not live,

In the past, where my greats were chained.

It's a good dang shame!

To be judged and ridiculed, without them knowing your name.

Just, by seeing your first layer.

See, her first layer is white, and my first layer is black

But the second layer, with the heart, mind, and soul is exact.

So, I guess I don't comprehend, how this is so lose win,

How being Black and beautiful, and having a strong mind is a sin.

When the acid rain fall upon our skin,

would you be able to see that I am black, and she is white then?

When only the pink skin and red blood is all the eyes can see.

Would you think that I am her or she is me?

Stop, being so content on the outside, when the content on the inside is what matters.

EMOTION

I recall our dark nights and dark tears.

I remember our silent cries and quiet fears.

I sometimes think about if I didn't have you through my hardest years,

Would I of made it this far, would I be where you are, and you here?

Time flies by, seconds wait for no one.

But the seconds I wasted, I regret, especially when they could have been with you.

My decision to go hundreds of miles away for school.

Promise I'd trade every ounce of education to be with you, when he chose to shoot.

Now it feels like a trade in.

Yes, I'm smarter now but deep down I'm draining.

And I'm changing, constantly, to be who you believed I could,

And I'm changing because I know I should, for me.

WORDS OF REFLECTION

YOUR TUNE

Mountains form by a thousand years, and

sometimes smiles form by a thousand tears, and

bravery is formed by a thousand fears.

Yet, our cries are ignored by a thousand ears.

Sometimes it seems that the world is mean;

and I know you feel like a peasant, no queen.

But through these feelings, remember you have a purpose.

Remember you're worth it, even though you're not perfect.

Just keep on working on yourself.

You must continue to build, continue to live,

continue to move, and sometimes groove.

Because dancing frees the soul, to the tune only you know.

And before you know it, you'll be going,

even if you doubted that you could go.

PRAISE HIM IN ADVANCE

This hard time has to be harder than the last time.

These tears are flowing harder than the last time.

This fake smile takes more out of me than the last time.

But seeing how my soul is darker than the last time.

I call on my Lord stronger than the last time;

and my hope is more hopeful than the last time.

Therefore, I am more faithful now, than I was the last time.

You see, the harder the time, the bigger the praise;

and I give my biggest praise on the better days.

Because I pray that he gives me guidance through my storms.

I'm beyond grateful when I reach my destination safely.

So even if my harder day is harder than the last time, I'll

Praise Him in advance.

TICK

Time ticks and bombs boom,

love heals later if not soon.

Now, I'm a nigger, not coon, or

maybe I still am, haven't seen a gold moon.

Because maybe if the gold moon shines,

the golden radiant rays will lighten

the hearts of all those who hate,

Me because of my color, not my attitude,

because of my strong and intelligent mind,

not my ignorance.

Because I chant, "BLACK POWER", not because I am powerless.

Because I speak, not silent, and I'm calm, not wilding.

Because I have control, not being controlled.

So sooner or later, when the golden moon shines, all lives will matter,

especially,

Black

Lives.

ODE TO MY MOTHER

Challenges of the challenge that formed every formation of her life.

Every hardship that could be imaged, made life hard for her.

Every ounce of sanity that any sane person has tried to escape her mind.

See life was this insane, that her sanity tried to hide.

Yet, she remains.

Yet,

She was able to teach me the game,

able to teach me to love my name,

able to teach me to stand, be independent without a man.

Able to defend myself and harm no one else.

I remember, they judged her for having my brothers and me,

and I judge her for her ability to raise a Queen and Kings.

Despite her

challenges.

FORBIDDEN FRUIT

The apples in the trees, the honey from the bees,

is like the potential on the inside,

the inside of me.

But my outside can't be ignored, accepted, or adored.

The inside can't grow, excel, or sore.

It's like one man said,

"Don't touch that apple in the tree, let em' hang,

and for fun and to entertain, set em' up in flames.

Set em' up for failure, keep them trapped down!

Make sure they kill each other, and one day they won't be around."

"That's the goal, and they know,

but through slavery and oppression

we've captured their race and their souls.

So, they ignore their truth,

they ignore their roots.

They don't know that they were Kings and Queens before we entered.

Make sure we keep that from the books!

Their history is what we make it!

We'll never accept them, but we'll fake it.

We'll have them work to the death to build our empires, until they expire, and when their offspring comes begging, we'll hire!"

BUT ME! I QUIT!

Respectfully, no fits!

I take complete pride in my black skin,

regardless of all institutionalized risks.

On the inside and out, I know that I AM beautiful,

even more now than I used to.

Because I know my roots,

proud of my ancestral truths.

Because as you continue to break us down, we continue to build you.

And if you don't think that we do, you should go back and read.

The pale man didn't build America

America was built by slavery.

WORDS OF REFLECTION

MIND ELEVATION

I don't understand why I'm feeling stuck,

feet melted to the pavement.

Heat from my soul traveling through my body, blessed I'm not brain dead.

"Is this only on me solely?" Or "Is someone else to blame?"

I ask myself those question, and I only come up with my name.

So yea, I guess being stuck is on me, so it's on me to be free.

Even if I must bend down and claw at the melted debris on my feet.

Since I'm blessed with today, it's another chance to try.

Break free from self-doubt, their doubts and lies.

My mental state can't suffer, for the mind is a terrible thing to waste.

If you do lose your mind, you'll become an oppressed mindless slave.

So my mind I'll cherish, stay strong,

and keep my head raised.

Mind Elevation over mind deflation.

A mind that matters is over everything.

TOGETHER

It's time to break these chains.

It's time to be known, not by my race, but my name.

It's time to be heard, by my laughs, not my tears;

time for life to be enjoyed, not feared.

Because, I'm tired of these times

where being black is a crime.

They said truth brings justice,

but it's never ours like we lied.

When my brothers die it goes unnoticed.

If the hand that holds the weapon is pale, the case turns the coldest.

But let it be a black hand, that's another black life in the white can.

Black lives filling graves and cells,

while white feet happily walk in the white sand.

Also, let me say that all blame isn't theirs.

Black lives invest in the black demise, we too, have a share.

Because some of us choose to be controlled, even if better we know.

We walk outside in shorts and sandals, when we clearly see the snow.

That's backwards and reverse is what I'm tired of and I mean it.

A world with no black lives is what they want and they see it.

Because we're painting that picture with daily, "never forgotten" and "miss you".

Children being raised without Kings, and to me, that's an issue.

I can't express enough, how it's time, to appreciate our lives first.

We can't complain how they kills us, because we're killing ourselves worse.

So yea, it's time to break these chains.

Flourish from the rain, you lose some and we've been losing.

But believe in how much we can gain.

Together.

THE CALM

Deep breaths, breathe in.

Ignore thoughts that said you'll never win.

Keep trying, move forward.

Only God can say when the fight is over.

Stand strong and realize that each day is a new chance as long as you're alive.

Keep faith high and doubt down,

remember before the storm, there will be no sound.

Just the calm, preparations.

Remember patience can only come from waiting.

We will overcome.

They say it's not over until the fat woman sings, and she hasn't sung.

So,

Until then, I'll raise my fists.

Speak BLACK POWER, to every witness.

You can hate my skin, beautiful color,

my sisters and brothers.

Mark my words, like you've marked our lives.

Racist bombs dropped, didn't kill us all, just opened our eyes.

With Mind Elevation and some patience, we will win.

Been through hell for too long, this is coming to an end!

BLACK ROSE

Should I view it as a blessing or a curse,

To be the last rose picked not first.

The longer I stay, the longer I live.

The longer I thrive and heal.

Yet, the longer I stay and the roses around me are picked,

the longer I feel less beautiful, important, and real.

Time after time, season by season,

I remain attached to my roots, unaware of the reason.
Could it be thorns that pricks the pickers fingers,

or the scent of what's unappealing, around me that lingers.

Is a petal or two missing, or are my petals not as red?

Is my outside finally turning the color of my inside, for my inside feel dead.

As more time passed, and I am attached for another season, I finally realize that my

petals are Black, and being a

Black Rose

is the reason.

WORDS OF REFLECTION

GENERATIONAL CYCLE

I want to declare my declaration,

that I am beautiful the way I am.

I can stand strong and powerful,

as a contained human or an unleashed animal.

And to say that I am less than, to me is fallible.

You think you can predict my predicate,

based on my skin color.

And that can be the only subject if you make it, it doesn't have to be another.

Inside can be brighter than the sun, but just because my outside is darker than night.

You keep the chains on our mind, so we don't put up a fight.

But see knowledge is the key, I unlocked those chains.

I know that I am more than my black skin and I'm aware of your games.

Black on black crime, brothers killing their brothers,

Before his brother killed him, he turned her into a mother.

I was taught, don't tear nobody when they're down.

But collectively we still are, and ya'll still tearing.

Hunting us for our dark skin,

skin us alive and our culture ya'll wearing.

Generational cycle.

REVOLUTION GENESIS

Revolution starts in the mind, when the soul is exhausted.

Revolution begins to find the truth, when the truth has been lost in,

the web of lies, lies entangled through time.

Revolution begins to unveil the sight, because

the sight has been blind.

For years, they showed that some lives matter, as long as the skin isn't black.

For years we've been killed by the same people that swore to protect.

Constitution neglects, laws enacted, to keep us where we're at.

In poverty and dependent on a system, with basically no blacks.

But what should we expect? Lives intended to pick and build.

Nothing can truly save us, except us.

We are our truest shield.

Only knowledge will build us, and only then will we pick one another.

Revolution starts in the mind to find the truth of the beautifully colored.

PROMOTION

I'm not sure why they're influencing our Queens to only promote their bodies,

Never their mind.

Trying to keep us mentally locked down, as if being NATURALLY beautiful, is a crime.

Justice system is the judge,

hope is the hopelessness in the gravel.

You see,

anybody can twerk on camera as long as the girl desire.

Anticipating likes or comments,

that's what sets her heart on fire.

But with the body being what it is, and

shared by literally every women on earth.

What will you do to be different?

Though one butt may be bigger or the breast on her chest.

It is the anatomy of every woman.

So, how will you be different?

Go beyond the body, into the mind

And show the world,

What your mind can do.

LOVE SURROUNDS

Love surrounds me so much that I know I'm loved.

Yet, lonely calls my name.

Not lonely as with nobody,

but lonely as my soul is alone.

My soul bare. Hidden tears.

Broken hearts. Deadly fears.

So, I sit silent. Hold in my lonely soul as for no one to know.

Because after all, love surrounds me.

And my love surrounds them.

So what love that heals, should be denied because of how I feel?

It can't.

I'm only the one that holds the peace together.

Although holding hurt in makes my mental shatter.

Broken down. Permanent frowns.

If only I could slip into the slipper of glass, and beautiful gown.

But, my life isn't a fairytale.

And I can't yell. And I can't scream.

But maybe, that's all I need.

But it's constant love surrounding,

So I smile because I'm the reminder.

That we won't be broken.

WORDS OF REFLECTION

GOLDIE LOCKS

The people who choose to find themselves are liberated.

While those who drown in negative despair will perish.

Because evil will take control over your mind.

Thus, take control of you.

Be strong and hold on, even if in the world, you're alone.

Be kind, love, and help others who are broken.

Because when your voice is spoken,

you will be heard.

When you are free to dream, your reality is what you make it.

"...and until then fake it."

As they say, but I won't encourage.

For you'll be as lost as the blonde girl breaking beds and stealing porridge.

HEAVY

Heart hanging heavy.

Sometimes it feels as if the organs that blesses life,

will be the reason that I cease to.

I constantly hear that if it's not broke don't fix it.

Still haven't heard how to fix it if it's broken.

Shattered.

On the edge of oblivion.

And oblivion is my world sometimes.

I can't see how I will heal without you.

But that's what faith is, something you can't see.

And my faith is infinite.

AUNTIE

Being away missing my babies grow.

The reason, one day I hope they know.

Is it right to sacrifice this time to ensure their development.

To become more successful now, I must, so they won't have to struggle as we did.

When we were kids.

But I miss them.

All their hugs and kisses.

To: Deon, Sy, Tay, Asa, Leah, JayCeon, Junior, and Seneca unborn I'm

sorry Auntie was missing.

Missing your hugs and kisses.

But for your future sake, I will miss you.

By my bed, grab the tissue.

When my eyes pour by the thought of you.

I love you, I love you, I love you, I love you, I

love you, I love you, I love you. I love you.

To each one of my KINGS and QUEEN.

Auntie miss you.

MI KENNY AMOR

When I walked in, my mother's skin,

was as cold as her soul.

Frozen in,

a time when his words and presence was near.

In her dreams, she never dreamed of her biggest fear.

And me, well my soul almost slipped away.

Only moments after the bomb entered my ears,

on the same day.

How could I continue in a world, that when I came into,

you were already here.

Had a year worth of laughs and tears.

Ya'll already had a bond, before my life begun.

And from my first day, you were her son and my sun.

My light through the darkness that we endured.

Blessed that I was able to find peace, although for a broken heart

there's no cure.

LA'TONYA RENEE

I preach your love and compassion because one can only

speak from experience.

I preach in your favor because you are favorable.

You are remarkable and inexplicably extraordinary.

The amount of my life that I dedicate to you is 100 percent.

You never abandoned me although the option became present

on numerous occasions.

Mother, you're amazingly amazing, and infamously famous,

I'll always be your baby that's now a lady.

Which I owe to the way that you raised me.

Riches neglected us, we inherited struggles and poverty.

But it is your strength on this battle field that made me who I am.

For you I will kill.

For you I will heal.

Through any personal battles I confront,

so that I will always be whole and strong,

when you need me to hold, you my dear.

My biggest fear, is not making you smile and proud.

I promise I'll work hard for a thousand years straight,

to present you with the crown, that you deserve.

Because although life is hard

and our family pulled death's card.

Together we will defeat all because you are our leader.

Who leads us with God first, family second.

WE will prosper because no weapon.

Will break you, therefore us.

Mommy I trust,

in you.

Regardless of what we've been through.

Just smile and be positive, because life could be worse.

So, lets only envision tomorrow,

not the desire to reverse.

The hands of time for no seconds,

for this life is a lesson.

We didn't have the money or material, but I had you.

My Mother,

My Queen,

My truest and purest blessing.

    LaTonya Renee

WORDS OF REFLECTION

STILL EXIST

Sparkling mist falling upon the eyes of the beholder.

Staring as I'm looking up, mist making my sight colder.

Soul astonished that you'll always be the oldest, yet I'm older.

Remember the initial thought of not wanting to live longer.

Time elapse,

my hands clasped,

holding tight, but perhaps.

I should free the Black dove, allow the wings to flap.

Afraid that in the future it'll become trapped.

Sight too focused on the light, move towards it, and ZAP!

They say,

blacker the merrier.

Yet, being black isn't merry,

blacks we bury and debt we carry.

So, I guess the blacker, the scarier.

Since we should be afraid,

that if we J-walk or litter, it could be our last day.

Yet, he can go on a killing spree,

be tased and one day, set free.

Should I wish I had pale skin?

Never.

Because black is beautiful and symbolizes strength.

Who you know can be hung, burned, and hated so strong but still exist?

I appreciate all people, but I won't be oblivious,

to blacks still being enslaved and discriminated against.

THE PRODUCT OF A LIE

They say lies hurt, yet they lie,

passionate lies on the bed side.

Words spoken, but truth choking,

can't be told, so they hurting.

Because they said lies hurt, yet they lie,

hurting others, lies multiply.

Losing meaning, forfeiting purpose.

No one can answer, "Was it worth it?"

Because they say all lie except two.

I promise one is me, can you promise two is you?

Guarding my soul for the promise land,

but my heart could be yours, don't you understand?

Granted,

sometimes my emotions show bare,

words, "I don't care",

heart cold for sixty seconds and smile not there.

But you see, they say all lie, except two.

My soul knows I'm one, dubious of you as two.

Because when my emotions are bare, I'm hurting, and the hurt is

the product of a lie.

THE BLACK DEALER

It's a dirty shame, but who's to blame?

For life is a gamble, who's the dealer in this game?

For the rules only apply, to the downed souls that cry.

The dealer hears, but too focused on the multiply.

To double their commerce, between the rules and the dealer, who's worse?

But I think...

That the dealers made the rules.

Number one, make sure every situation is lose, lose.

For all the niggers and the coons.

For the thugs and black girls, butts like a bamboo.

More blacks incarcerated, more black teens having babies, more black men in the ground.

To every white cop, gun them down!

Yep, that will be rule number two.

I wonder what number three will make them do.

Strip away their hope and lets add a pun for fun.

Let hope be the queen, strip her down to only her body, never letting her true mind and purpose be seen.

And let her raise her children to be worse.

For it starts with the mother, regardless of her hurt.

Because she hurts.

ONCE MORE

Water absorbed into my pores.

Inhale, exhale, inhale once more.

My eyes open, realizing I'm still here.

Another second to do good. For minutes isn't promised nor years.

So, what to do when all but your mind is against you.

What to do? What to do?

When the words, "I love you", loses meaning,

everybody leaving and ignore me screaming.

Heart broken, breathing heavy, body leaning.

Wish I'd known in the beginning, the outcome.

Would I've embarked on this journey, or chose to skip this lesson?

But all is a blessing, because although I hurt,

I am able to,

 inhale, exhale, inhale once more.

Realizing I'm still here and blessed.

SISTA

"Sista, you've been on my mind. Oh sista, you're one of a kind.

Oh sista, I'm someone and you're somebody to."**

Sista, you've been on my mind.

Sista, you've been on my mind, and through this time.

I want to remind you to keep your faith up,

you know what the world can't touch.

Ignore the stereotypes of yourself, ignore the bad, no luck,

is needed, if you believe it.

That you're a Queen so you're winning.

Even if you feel like you're lost,

pick your head up, it's free, no cost.

God planned this battle.

He knew you'd be rattled.

But your strength is deep within.

So, say no goodbye's, as a true friend.

Smile, light up the world that feels darkened around you.

Inspire your sister.

Say "You've been on my mind.", as I told you.

**Spielberg, Steven dir. "The Color Purple". Perf. Danny Glover and Whoopi Goldberg. Warner Bros./Amblin Entertainment, 1985.

Miss Celie's Blues (Sister): Quincy Jones/Lionel Richie/Tod Temperton

WORDS OF REFLECTION

REALITY

Why do we kill because of colors,

when we're getting killed for being colored?

Why are we angry at each other, instead of helping one another?

Why is the world at our feet?

Why should, could, or would I

pretend to be clueless to the facts.

Ignorant to the past, that is present in today.

They can kill my race, without serving one day.

They can laugh at his burial, I'm standing here telling you,

something's wrong.

Because what isn't right, is constantly losing the fight.

The votes are rigged, don't even use black pens.

But blue, and those is blue aren't true.

Not protectors but neglectors.

Like Peter the pelican ate pecan pie.

I be so tongue tied, tongue dried,

dehydrated of blood, like my soul died.

Yet, I cry not a tear.

For glory will be ours as Mr. Legand sang.

For the times I dialed 911 from my hood and the phone rang.

No respondent, thus no response,

plenty lives could of been saved, yet, they're gone.

Guess black lives:

cry invisible tears,

bleed invisible blood,

give invisible love,

cherish invisible memories.

Or

white lives, ignore black tears,

black blood,

black love,

black memories.

Which is my reality?

THE GREATER RISK

I know my mind is strong, although sometimes I break.

Sometimes my mind overloads, which cause my body to shake.

Like the earthquake.

Two things can separate, by two tectonic plates.

Natural occurrences, natural disasters.

Maybe sometimes it's natural to break.

Break away from the place where the motion is constant.

Rather you feel movement or not.

But when it does get to higher ground and regardless,

I'm marching to the top.

Mark my words.

Because this is a cause that I'm willing to risk everything on.

This is a voice that I'm willing to speak.

This is a vision that I'm willing to see.

A journey I'm willing to walk.

If it starts with an idea, I'll have the thought.

If a heart is what it takes to bring it to life,

I'm willing to sacrifice mine.

If the scent of change must be smelled, I'll inhale.

And when darkness inevitably arrives, my mind will prevail.

STRAINED

Giving them the satisfaction that, their tunnel vision is the only vision.

Cases don't go to trial, but I witness, the trap we're in.

The weed is the lie,

the money is the deceit,

the freaks is the weak,

the gun is the plot.

They allow them, to easily be in our possession,

because they know we'll grab it, carry it, and shoot it,

causing another black life to be useless.

So now my,

mental is strained, in a million ways,

feels like I've lived 400 years in three days.

They say what's understood, don't have to be explained.

But I say what's hard to understand, should be.

Only three people I trust with my life, including myself would be four.

My Lord, my mother, and finally my angel Kenny Amor.

Mind in a constant cycle of unrest,

soul and body constantly chanting with signs in protest.

They say Black Lives Matter,

but only the white man chatters.

For it's he who discuss the rules around his table, and

they wonder why we're "unstable".

THE GENERATIONAL CURSE

Bond together by hopelessness yet divided by the lack of intelligence.

The lack of knowledge that all people of different races and beliefs can live civilly with one another without the hate and despair.

The young girl who's pregnant with her second child, she was maturing and developing inside of her mother sixteen years prior.

The fact that sixteen years prior while she was maturing and developing her mother was in the daughter's shoes.

With one child on her hip feeling blue with no clue.

While she's carrying and bearing her mother was 32,

partying living the life as if 10 years was subtracted from her age.

Because by 22 she had three children on her own,
placing men and not God upon her throne.

Now we see three generations of teen mothers with no fathers.

Young lives full of diapers, pacy's, and bottles.

Bottles, while the babies drink their milk, momma drink her liquor.

Let man after man in so her scars get deeper.

Funny how granny, momma, and daughter walked, lived, and breathed the same footsteps.

Not one had the thought to place their own prints in the sand.

Not one thought to choose THE MAN over a man,

open a book not their legs, look in the mirror and said I CAN.

The young boy who's posted on the corner at fourteen.

He weighs 150 pounds but if he steps on a scale it would read 160.

Ten pounds added from the weapons, drugs, and dirty cash,

pants hanging off his a*s.

When he makes a transaction, he does the math in his head.

Yet I'm not sure why he can't solve the problem by subtracting his being from the street

and add it to a classroom, divide the negativity by many and multiply the positive by plenty.

But see, he's the son of a woman whose daughter is pregnant at 16.

Only men he seen coming and going was literally Cumming then going.

The men entered his mother's bedroom at night and gone by the morning.

So, he thinks that the man he's becoming, is one in which he has no choice of.

Don't let me forget to mention, that he's the father of a baby, the mother 15, and has no love.

She only believes what she sees, and her mother had her at 16, and her mother walked in her mother's shoes.

The son only believes what he sees, and he never seen his father.

Living life playing by the generational curse rules.

WORDS OF REFLECTION

POW POW

Pow! Pow!

Is the sound I hear out the window.

It startles me not because it's a sound that I know.

Raised in poverty, where it's rare to dream.

Only concern is waking the next day to see.

And if you make it, you try not to waste it.

Another day another dollar,

if you don't make it then you take it.

Remember once I was 16 they robbed him and later he came back.

Us 7 chilling in front of my house, seen the gun

our first thought was to run.

Reviewed 16 years in twenty seconds.

I just thank God that we made it.

See, our lives were spared,

but similar tears we shared.

For C.Martin, Kevin, and Marcus whose lives isn't here.

Tinky rest in peace, Shaun money we holding it down.

All started in the 8th grade when Chris Drinkard drowned.

So I been scared since day one,

but I pray through day two,

and all night I hear the shots,

but dream on is what I do.

Pow! Pow!

Is the sound I hear out my window.

Close my eyes and say, "Here they go."

My hood was the Crips,

down the street were the Bloods.

Blue flag in their left pocket,

and their hand was the gun.

Triggers they pulled,

marijuana is what they lit.

Police, they had no love,

yea, that's where I'm from.

Pow! Pow!

Is the sound I heard through my door.

Rain was pouring this night,

even harder than before.

Walked down the street, seen his brains on the pavement.

I just seen him earlier but be careful who you play with.

My hood was relentless in its prime.

All the gangsters are expired or celled down doing time.

Through, all the blood, sweat, and tears

just wish dreams was possible, especially for my peers.

Barely hit high school, before he was holding that glock.

Before she became a mother,

becoming even harder to struggle.

Before he hit that line,

not working, but he doing time.

Wasn't worried about graduating, only focused on the grind.

Said this the life he wanted but to himself he lied.

Just didn't want to seem weak and low in the Gangster's eyes.

FORGIVE

Seems we're at a standstill like bad traffic.

Want me to have a mental breakdown, cranial attic.

I see black children playing, wondering if they'll be one of the bodies laying.

Viewed as the vampire soul sucker in society, so who'd be doing the slaying?

Memories flash back because we played.

Half buried, half chained, I'll call that slayed.

"Forgive them father for they know not what they do."

I read those words from the Bible,

heard it at Sunday's recital.

Confusion and questions create waves in the calm sea,

And I'll ask the ones that create the tidal.

Like, what did my people do, to be disgusting by you and hated?

No apologies in 400 years, far past belated.

MIRROR

Looking into the mirror,

I see the pain that lies beneath.

Yet a smile lies on my face, so the world can't see.

The hurt that burns to the core,

my heart is healed, but it's still sore.

As I look into my eyes, I ask myself, "Is there more?"

More to the days that are limited.

Or should I cut them short, like Tookie did.

I had the thought in my younger days.

But what would gain, if I laid down to soon?

Thoughts like this send me to the moon.

No Mary in my system, but my mind gets high, like I lift up.

Say a prayer as I look in the mirror and reflect on myself.

Just thankful that I have my knowledge and health.

The best thing I ever did was not commit suicide.

The thought ran through my mind, when the tears filled my eyes.

Thankful that my Lord is by my side because

He never put more on me that I can't handle.

Looking in the mirror,

I remember when I had the knife in my hand.

Life was breaking me down, and the thoughts of my dad.

Was overbearing, emotions were stingy, I was not sharing.

So, I held them in, not one friend, would understand why I'm burying.

Myself alive, suffocating like j. Holiday.

Can't be selfish with my breathe, cause my debt He paid.

HIDDEN DEPTHS

As I look into my poster, realizing life is getting older.

I wonder if the deeper I go, will it get colder?

Deeper in thoughts, hidden depths is what I call it.

Would I be able to handle the truth?

Or write this book?

Would I be able to face myself and take a look?

If I got one peak would I notice me?

Is the hidden depths of myself someone I could meet?

The hard truth buried, the easy lies is what lies on the outside.

Buried deep within, deep in the hidden depths, but can be seen deep into my eyes.

The line between selfish and self-less, is as thin as love and hate.

Like knowing something is bad,

but craving the good taste.

I write what's on my mind, my thoughts can't be wasted.

My thoughts become forever,

even when memory comes in and erase it.

There's a thin line between love and hate.

Even thinner between defeat and victory.

Apparently lies predict our present,

but what's more apparent, is that's there's a mystery.

Like, every religion basically says not to judge others,

but you look down on a religion that's not yours.

Just remember that we're all man, trying to live life before God pulls our card.

Cause at that second: no waiting, no talking, no singing.

No ands nor but. No begging, no luck.

No amount of money can buy you more time, after you've been touched.

So, when our Father reaches down, and calls home my soul,

mourn me not, just always remember my words like a song.

MORSE

I heard money is the new God, we bow down to the paper.

Give our praise to the truly invaluable, worship what is completely fallible.

When you give your life to this deceit, you're far from being free.

The industrial revolution destroyed our land, politics ruined our lives.

We're told to only live to make paper, and to me that's a lie.

What about the memories and laughs?

Yes, the poorest can fulfil the most.

Raise your glass if you choose to live, and join me with this toast.

They say it takes a village, but it must first be built.

The land can't save us, if the soil hasn't been healed.

Once the soul has regained its promise, its hope, and freedom.

The roots will again take hold, and from it, the truth will flourish.

More eyes will blink,

Because their living.

Sending the signal of victory, call this code,

Morse.

THE EVIL EFFECT

When evil speaks, hatred leaks.

Through the blood and veins of the mentally weak.

When evil hears, innocence is feared,

so black babies are murdered, guess their fears are cleared.

Charges are dropped, or no wrong doing is mentioned.

Three strikes, we're out,

never played, just in the dugout sitting.

Ref calls the shots, and he says, "Cops shoot!"

When they go to the courts, they pass the blame from me to you, like alley-oop.

So you can call me persistent or call me loony

for spending years and dedicating my life to figure out how we're still losing.

Victims of war, of greed, of power.

Victimized every minute, second, and hour.

Physically abused,

Mentally tormented.

Spiritually mislead.

Our truth deliberately missing.

Identity kidnapped, lives held for ransom.

But they said the brightest diamond is produced by the most pressure.

Situations perpetuating.

Yet, patiently waiting for good days.

Still waiting.

And I know sometimes the truth can be disturbing,

but think about what you're learning.

WORDS OF REFLECTION

TO BELONG

It's always something, like it's never just nothing.

Stressing out got my mind going crazy and fussing.

I pray to keep my mind,

I pray to survive.

I pray that I don't die, before opening my eyes.

Because nights can bring sorrow, days can bring the pain.

I understand how it feels to lose it all again and again.

I just have to stay strong,

focused on the outcome.

I'm focused on my breakthrough,

 better days here I come.

Because,

with all due respect,

I have to get this off my chest.

I'm tired of you looking at me like my skin is cursed,

not blessed.

I'm tired of you talking at me like common sense,

neglected my race.

I'm tired of you telling me I don't belong, like

we didn't build this place.

CONVENIENCE

My sister read me her poem describing being loved at others convenience.

I told her that I understood the feeling then, and now, I still feel it.

Heart soft in many places, although harder in more.

The hardness formed through the process of healing,

could have sunk, but I landed at shore.

I give my word that I love you,

something about you I adore.

But my intuition steady itching,

either it's good or it's bad.

Is it my hand or my vein?

something I wish I never had.

That line has become a cliché, but so has lying.

My God delivered me on my birthday, and I came in as a lion!

Your sudden outbursts,

let me tell you how this is going to go.

You're going to stop speaking down on me

like you're high and I'm low.

Show respect or show no love,

no in between or no middle.

My soul big and my heart is bigger,

although my physical is little.

But what's not little is my bite,

don't let me bite down on you.

Because I'll open up and swallow,

and not chew, like you're soup.

So, lets just make your sudden outbursts less sudden,

and we'll be cool.

I hope these words were convenient.

THE CALL

Contemplating on why we're waiting to be who we're meant to be.

Aware of deceit planned to keep us blinded,

where we can't see.

Mentally shocked,

by the physical knocks and kicks to our culture.

We weren't the country married to America,

yet they came and fucked us, fucking adulterers.

Now we're the stepchild without Cinderella,

no fairies or magical dust.

Just locked in the basement chained,

our collective mind has no aim.

Before we can dream, we must first awaken.

I'm sure they expect us to stay down,

but I'm even more sure they're mistaken.

They kill the many of us to satisfy the few of them.

But I thought it was supposed to be, "sacrifice the few for the many".

But it's really about their convenience, they scheming.

Now, the grand scheme is to survive by any means.

Necessary and it's a necessity to awaken before the next generations open their eyes.

My words can be read and understood, everyone's welcome.

But this is a call to black lives.

FORWARD

Sometimes I feel we're at a standstill.

Open wounds still fresh through the years, I thought time healed.

Broken hearts, broken homes, and broken promises.

Sometimes I feel that we're still living excluded and misunderstood like the Amish did.

And do, but what's true, is that we're supposed to be moving forward with progression,

moving forward with no neglecting,

moving forward with no oppression.

Like Dr. King said before the weapon, was drew that ended the peace that he was repping.

I have a dream that one day freedom will ring, equality will metaphorically become the fat lady that sings.

To the tune of inclusion, the tune of no more blacks being abused and the tune of Dr. King's voice.

They say patience is a virtue, but I need this here, to be rushed.

For how many more years must I pray, that Dr. King's legacy will become a lifestyle?

For how many more years must I pray, that we can move forward down the right aisle?

Forever grateful for the accomplishments that has been achieved by his voice.

If he'd been silent, we wouldn't have moved forward much.

So, for him and us, I'll make some noise!

HER-STORY

I was born by the river in a tent like Seal said,

been running since that day and ever since.

Mind racing, Ms. Felix couldn't catch up.

Tired of crying cause blacks gets no love!

Bodies and after bodies pilling up, like bad traffic.

If we born from the womb, but not human, tell me how that happened!

Look at my skin like I'm witchcraft, dark magic.

Spielberg didn't tell us to be oppressed and said action!

We're not acting.

But you act like you're superior, and I'm inferior to you.

Raised by single mothers, because our fathers, put their hands up and you shoot.

White chalk trace their bodies, while the white killer goes home.

Black blood been on white hands, since back before you forced the Indians to go.

Trial of tears, trials of bodies, left behind wherever you go.

If his-story repeats itself, well soon, his-story is going to stop being made.

Because this story is mine, and her-story is the name.

Respect our lives, respect our skin, God created us all.

Been up on your high horse for too many hundreds of years, it's time for you to fall.

Take you down a level or two, better yet, three is more like it.

Going to stop repeating ourselves soon, the next step is fighting.

I can symbolize non-violence, but you're assassinating that image.

And if it comes to the point of "by any means",

you'll be getting what you're wishing.

Four, three, two, one

Times up. No more asking.

FOUNTAIN

I'm starting to sense this pattern that my true feelings don't matter.

I'm starting to hear you telling me what you think I want to, and to me that's an issue.

As you tell me more words, I'm beginning to hear slurs.

Hopefully soon, you won't be completely ignored, because the bullshit is for the birds.

My heart loves you so, but my mind is starting to neglect these heartfelt emotions.

Never again will my heart call the shots, so regardless of the notion,

that I love you.

I will be hesitant to leave but what I will do, is close the door if you continue.

To only allow me to hear from your mouth what you think I want to.

Feeling like I'm getting taken for granted,

and I'm sorry if I'm ranting.

But you had me too high in the clouds, and slowly I'm landing.

Going to hit the ground running, no turning back, even I want to.

No apologies will be able to erase the words, especially after I told you.

Not to lie to me ever, I can handle the truth even if burns.

I keep repeating this lesson to you, they say some never learn.

Not sure how much time I must sacrifice, just because of this one word: Love

Fountain of youth doesn't exist, and even if it does.

I wouldn't touch a drip with my finger, even if the thought lingers, because to go back is to erase, and I don't desire either.

So I'll just continue forward, with you or without.

It really all depends on the next few words out of your mouth.

If I continue to hear only the things you think that I want to.

I'll pop that single pill and cure all of our issues.

LAST WORDS

A wise Queen once said," When you're young you have all of these ideas about how you want your life to be. You have dreams and goals, but you never really know how life is going to play out for you." That Queen took part in the introduction of this book about Black Excellence. Tiesha, Chanekka and I met many years ago and we all three have overcome many different life challenges. For you, the reader, I am sure you have had many ups and downs, but always be thankful you are even able to open this book and grow your mind.

This book about the melanin experience is about the rollercoaster ride we as Kings and Queens have to live with on a daily basis. The purpose of this book is to remind you, you are made of gold. Your history is pure. Your struggle is not unnoticed. Your heart is heavy from the news. Every day, you turn on your televisions, only to find out another king or queen's life has been taken. By the very people we pay to protect us. You see that we are killing each other in the streets as well. It is hard to understand, but a change is coming. This book serves as a purpose to console you, and let you know that you are not alone.

Your melanin is feared because they see what you are capable of, before you do. Greatness, is what you are made of. You are beautiful and you shine every single day. I pray that this Black Girl Magic that Chanekka, my beloved sister, has bestowed upon you makes you get up and look in the mirror and remind yourself that you are royalty. God made you with nothing less than perfection. We want nothing more than for you to finish this book, go out into the world and rock your Melanin Experience. Keep your head held high, shoulders back with a smile on your face. You. Are. Magic.

Brothers and Sisters, Kings and Queens,

The Trio LOVES you. The Trio is WITH you.

Love always, "The Trio" - Chanekka, Kristin and Tiesha

ACKNOWLEDGEMENTS

*God: First and foremost, it is He who I give all my praise. For His name stands alone. What would I be without his grace, mercy, forgiveness, love and guidance. Nowhere. So, for these reasons and his blessings of my life. I give all glory to God.

*My Queen: My reason, my heart, my mother, LaTonya Renee Pullens. Thank you for being a mother through countless obstacles and never once abandoning me or my brothers. Your strength continues as you raise Kenny's children. It amazes me how your faith and love never wavers. I dedicate who I am to you solely. Period.

*Brothers: William, Devonte, and D'tearius Southern. Seneca Oden Jr, Christopher Bell and Angelo Gleaves. I thank you all for loving me unconditionally and creating some of the happiest moments in my life. Thank you all for encouraging me and believing in my ability. I love you all tremendously.

*Sisters: Tiesha McKenzie and Kristin Riddle. Thank you two queens so much for your powerful words in this book. When I initially asked you two to write a part, I never could have imagined the gold you would create. Then again, I shouldn't be surprised right? I am very appreciative and grateful to have been blessed with the two best friends, two best sisters, to share this journey through this life with. I love you queens!

*Franklin: My king on earth. Thank you. You are truly a great man and I love you purely. You have been nothing less than supportive since my first word was written. It was only God that brought you to my life. I love you and this is dedicated to you. I love you my hazel eyed king.

*Special Friends: Adrienne Walker and Kiara Jones. I'd like to take this time to acknowledge the strength and persistence of you two queens. You two have been amazing friends and always there for me when I needed a helping hand or an ear. I've known you both since before high school, but our bond was cemented through our adventurous college experience. Thank you both truly for being amazing and special friends.

MY ANGEL

Wow. Can you believe it? Our second book. Who knew I'd have so much to say? I'm sometimes fascinated yet humbled how life works out. How the challenging chapters in our lives would result in chapters in books. That's how I know that a much greater, a much more powerful force is in control. I miss you more than life itself. But I must and I will continue to find an inch of peace a day. An inch of understanding and acceptance. Of forgiveness. I find solace in the complete fact that you knew and know that you are loved. Especially by our immediate family. Siblings, mother, and your children. We cherished you then, we cherish you now. We loved you then and we love you now. And we all miss you forever. Continue to rest peacefully and powerfully. To my only big brother, my person, my best friend, my king. Ke'Lonzo Deontez Pullens Sr. Kenny Mi Amor.

PLEDGE

I, _____, pledge to take the necessary steps to Mind Elevation. I will instill knowledge and positive energy in those around me. I will think of positive outcomes to all negative situations. I will instill positive messages and create a positive life for the children in my life. I pledge to take my part in changing lives. On my honor, I will help in Chasing Prosperity!

ABOUT THE AUTHOR

Chanekka Chae' Pullens is a 2015 graduate of Middle Tennessee State University. She received her Bachelors Degree in Political Science with a double minor in History and International Relations. She self-published her first book, "The Book About M.E.: Mind Elevation" in 2015. She currently resides in Tennessee where she has commenced writing her third book.

www.ingramcontent.com/pod-product-compliance
Lightning Source LLC
Chambersburg PA
CBHW051701090426
42736CB00013B/2480